Mastering Chip

A Comprehensive Guide to Creating Intricate Designs.

Albert Milan

Table of Content

CHAPTER ONE
Introduction to Chip Carving

Whether you're an experienced woodworker seeking to broaden your skill set or a novice enthusiast eager to delve into the world of chip carving, this book serves as your entryway into an engaging and fulfilling craft.

Chip carving is a traditional woodworking technique that involves removing small chips of wood from a surface to create intricate patterns and designs. With just a few basic tools and some practice, you can transform humble pieces of wood into stunning works of art.

In this book, we'll start by delving into the history of chip carving and exploring the tools and materials you'll need to get started. From there, we'll cover fundamental techniques, such as the three-cut chip and straight-walled chip, before diving into more advanced methods for creating depth, texture, and dimension in your carvings.

But chip carving is more than just a technical skill—it's also a form of artistic expression. Throughout these pages, you'll learn how to design and execute your own patterns, from simple geometric shapes to intricate floral motifs and beyond. Along the way, we'll discuss design principles, troubleshooting tips, and strategies for refining your carving skills.

Whether you're interested in creating functional pieces like coasters and picture frames or decorative items like ornaments and figurines, this book has something for you. With plenty of projects for practice and inspiration, you'll soon be on your way to creating beautiful chip-carved masterpieces of your own.

So sharpen your tools, grab a piece of wood, and let's dive into the world of chip carving together. The journey ahead promises to be both challenging and immensely rewarding, and I'm excited to be your guide every step of the way. Let's get carving!

Chip Carving Meaning

Chip carving is a woodworking technique that involves the removal of small chips or pieces of wood from a flat surface to create intricate designs and patterns. This decorative carving method typically utilizes a small, sharp knife or chisel to make precise cuts, often forming geometric shapes, floral motifs, or stylized designs. Chip carving is known for its precision, simplicity, and elegance, making it a popular choice for decorating furniture, utensils, boxes, and other wooden objects.

History

The history of chip carving dates back centuries and spans across various cultures around the world. While it's challenging to pinpoint the exact origins of chip carving, evidence of this woodworking technique can be found in many ancient civilizations.

One of the earliest known examples of chip carving comes from the Viking Age, where intricate designs were carved into wood surfaces, such as furniture, utensils, and architectural elements. These carvings often featured geometric patterns and stylized motifs, reflecting the artistic sensibilities of the time.

In medieval Europe, chip carving flourished as both a decorative and functional art form. Skilled craftsmen carved elaborate designs into wooden chests, panels, and religious artifacts, adding embellishments to everyday objects and sacred items alike.

During the Renaissance period, chip carving continued to evolve, with artisans incorporating more intricate designs and experimenting with new techniques. The rise of woodworking guilds and the spread of printed pattern books helped to popularize chip carving as an accessible form of artistic expression.

In the 19th and 20th centuries, chip carving experienced a resurgence of interest, particularly in regions with strong folk art traditions, such as Scandinavia and Central Europe. Woodworkers and hobbyists embraced chip carving as a way to preserve cultural heritage and express their creativity through the medium of wood.

Today, chip carving remains a beloved woodworking technique practiced by artisans, hobbyists, and craftsmen around the world. While its origins may be ancient, its timeless appeal continues to inspire new generations of woodworkers to explore the art of carving intricate designs into wood surfaces, keeping the tradition alive for centuries to come.

Essential Tools

To embark on your chip carving journey, you'll need a few essential tools. Here's a list of the basics:

Chip Carving Knife: A sharp, narrow-bladed knife specifically designed for chip carving. Look for a knife with a comfortable handle and a thin, razor-sharp blade that allows for precise cuts.

Bench Knife or Chisel: A bench knife or chisel with a straight blade is useful for making straight cuts and removing larger sections of wood. Choose a chisel with a comfortable handle and a sharp edge for optimal control.

Sharpening Supplies: Keeping your carving tools sharp is crucial for achieving clean cuts and crisp lines. Invest in sharpening stones or strops to maintain the sharpness of your knives and chisels.

Cutting Mat: A cutting mat provides a safe and stable surface for chip carving. Choose a self-healing cutting mat to protect your work surface and extend the lifespan of your tools.

Pencil and Ruler: These basic drafting tools are essential for sketching out your designs and marking guidelines on your wood surface before carving.

Sandpaper: Sandpaper in various grits (from coarse to fine) is essential for smoothing and refining your carved surfaces. Choose high-quality sandpaper to achieve a professional finish.

Safety Gear: Protect your hands and eyes with gloves and safety glasses while chip carving. Safety should always be a top priority when working with sharp tools and wood.

With these essential tools in hand, you'll be ready to start your chip carving projects with confidence. As you gain experience and tackle more complex designs, you may choose to expand your tool collection with additional specialty knives, chisels, and accessories.

Essential Materials

In addition to the essential tools, you'll need a few key materials to begin your chip carving projects:

Wood: Choose a suitable wood species for chip carving, such as basswood, butternut, or pine. These types of wood are notably soft and carve with ease, rendering them perfect choices for those new to the craft. You can purchase pre-cut wood blanks or rough lumber to prepare your own carving surfaces.

Carving Blanks: Pre-cut wood blanks specifically designed for chip carving are available in various sizes and shapes, including squares, rectangles, and rounds. These blanks provide a convenient starting point for your projects and ensure a consistent thickness and quality of wood.

Finish: Applying a finish to your chip-carved pieces not only enhances their appearance but also protects the wood from moisture and wear. Choose a finish that suits your preference and the intended use of the finished piece, such as polyurethane, shellac, or oil-based varnish.

Sandpaper: As mentioned earlier, sandpaper in various grits is essential for smoothing and refining your carved surfaces. Start with coarse-grit sandpaper to remove any rough spots or tool marks, then progress to finer grits for a smoother finish.

Transfer Paper: Transfer paper or carbon paper is useful for transferring your design onto the wood surface before carving. Simply place the transfer paper between your design and the wood, then trace over the lines to transfer the image onto the wood.

Protective Gear: Ensure your safety while chip carving by wearing gloves to protect your hands from cuts and splinters, as well as safety glasses to shield your eyes from flying chips and debris.

Safety Precautions

Safety is paramount when engaging in chip carving or any woodworking activity. Below are crucial safety measures to adhere to:

Wear Safety Gear: Always wear appropriate safety gear, including gloves to protect your hands from cuts and splinters, and safety glasses to shield your eyes from flying wood chips and debris.

Use Sharp Tools: Keep your carving tools sharp to ensure clean cuts and reduce the risk of slips or accidents. Dull tools require more force to use, increasing the likelihood of injury.

Mind Your Fingers: Pay close attention to the positioning of your fingers and hands while carving. Keep your non-dominant hand well clear of the cutting edge, and use a secure grip on your carving tool to maintain control.

Work in a Controlled Environment: Carve in a well-lit and well-ventilated area with a stable work surface. Make sure your workspace is free from clutter and distractions to minimize the risk of accidents.

Respect the Grain: Be mindful of the direction of the wood grain while carving. Carving against the grain can cause tear-out and splintering, leading to accidents or damage to your workpiece.

Secure Your Workpiece: Use clamps or a vice to secure your workpiece firmly in place while carving. A stable workpiece reduces the risk of slips and ensures greater control over your carving tools.

Take Breaks: Carving requires focus and concentration, so take regular breaks to rest and refresh your mind and body. Fatigue can lead to lapses in attention and increased risk of accidents.

Clean Up Properly: Keep your workspace clean and organized to prevent trips, slips, and falls. Dispose of wood chips and debris regularly and store your tools safely when not in use.

CHAPTER TWO
Getting Started

Choosing The Right Wood

Choosing the right wood is crucial for successful chip carving. Here are some factors to consider when selecting wood for your projects:

Hardness: Opt for a wood species that is relatively soft and easy to carve, especially if you're a beginner. Basswood, butternut, and pine are popular choices for chip carving due to their softness and workability. Avoid woods that are too hard or dense, as they can be difficult to carve and may cause your tools to dull quickly.

Grain: Look for wood with a straight and even grain pattern, as this will make chip carving easier and more predictable. Avoid woods with irregular or interlocking grain, as they can cause tear-out and splintering, making it challenging to achieve clean cuts and smooth surfaces.

Texture: Consider the texture of the wood surface and how it will affect your carving. Smooth, fine-grained woods are ideal for intricate chip carving, while rough or coarse-grained woods may require more effort to carve and may not yield as detailed results.

Availability: Choose a wood species that is readily available and affordable in your area. Basswood is widely available at craft stores and online suppliers, making it a popular choice for chip carving enthusiasts. Alternatively, you can explore local hardwoods or reclaimed wood for unique and sustainable carving projects.

Size and Shape: Select wood blanks or boards that are appropriate for your intended project size and shape. Pre-cut wood blanks are available in various sizes and shapes, including squares, rectangles, and rounds, providing a convenient starting point for your carving projects.

Stability: Consider the stability and durability of the wood species you choose. Avoid woods that are prone to warping, splitting, or cracking, especially if you're carving functional items like utensils or decorative pieces intended for long-term use.

Preparing The Wood

Preparing the wood properly is essential for successful chip carving. Here's a step-by-step guide to preparing your wood surfaces for carving:

Select High-Quality Wood: Choose a suitable wood species for chip carving, such as basswood, butternut, or pine. Look for wood that is free from knots, cracks, and defects, as these can interfere with your carving and compromise the final result.

Cut to Size: If you're starting with rough lumber or larger boards, use a saw to cut the wood to the desired size and shape for your project. Alternatively, you can purchase pre-cut wood blanks in various sizes and shapes for convenience.

Sand the Surface: Use sandpaper to smooth the surface of the wood and remove any rough spots or imperfections. Start with a coarse-grit sandpaper (around 120 grit) to quickly remove material, then progress to finer grits (up to 220 grit or higher) for a smooth finish. Sanding the wood surface will not only improve its appearance but also make it easier to transfer and carve your designs.

Seal the Wood (Optional): Depending on the wood species and your personal preference, you may choose to seal the wood surface before carving. Applying a thin coat of sealer, such as shellac or sanding sealer, can help prevent the wood from absorbing moisture and make it easier to carve. Allow the sealer to dry completely before proceeding with carving.

Transfer Your Design: Use transfer paper or carbon paper to transfer your design onto the wood surface. Place the transfer paper between your design and the wood, then trace over the lines with a pencil or ballpoint pen to transfer the image onto the wood. Alternatively, you can draw your design directly onto the wood surface using a pencil and ruler.

Protect the Workpiece: Once your design is transferred, handle the wood with care to avoid smudging or damaging the transferred lines. Consider using a light touch when handling the wood, or place a piece of scrap paper over the transferred design to protect it from accidental smudges or marks.

CHAPTER THREE
Basic Chip Carving Techniques

Three Cut Chip

The three-cut chip is one of the fundamental techniques in chip carving, allowing you to create clean and precise triangular shapes. Here's how to execute the three-cut chip:

Marking the Design: Begin by marking the outline of the triangle you want to carve onto the wood surface using a pencil or marking knife. You can use a ruler to ensure straight lines and consistent angles.

Making the Stop Cut: With your chip carving knife, make a shallow cut along one side of the triangle outline, defining the edge of the chip. This cut is known as the "stop cut" and serves as a boundary for the chip.

Making the First Slant Cut: Position your knife at a 65-75 degree angle to the wood surface, with the cutting edge facing towards the center of the triangle. Begin making a diagonal cut from the outer edge of the triangle towards the stop cut. This cut should meet the stop cut, creating a triangular ridge of wood.

Making the Second Slant Cut: Repeat the process for the opposite side of the triangle. Position your knife at the same angle and make a diagonal cut towards the stop cut, meeting it to create another triangular ridge of wood.

Removing the Chip: Finally, carefully insert the tip of your knife into the center of the triangle and make a vertical cut down towards the base of the triangle, removing the triangular chip of wood cleanly from the surface. Use controlled pressure to ensure a clean cut without splintering or tearing the wood fibers.

Refining the Shape: After removing the chip, use your knife or chisel to clean up any rough edges or imperfections, ensuring that the edges of the triangle are crisp and defined.

Repeat as Needed: Repeat the process for each triangle in your design, adjusting the size and angle of the triangles as necessary to create the desired pattern.

Straight Walled Chip

The straight-walled chip is another fundamental technique in chip carving, commonly used to create straight lines and borders in your designs. Here's how to execute the straight-walled chip:

Marking the Design: Begin by marking the outline of the straight line or border you want to carve onto the wood surface using a pencil or marking knife. Use a ruler or straight edge to ensure the line is straight and even.

Making the Stop Cuts: With your chip carving knife, make two shallow cuts along the length of the marked line, defining the edges of the chip. These cuts are known as the "stop cuts" and serve as boundaries for the chip.

Removing the Wood: Position your knife perpendicular to the wood surface, with the cutting edge facing towards the center of the marked line. Begin removing wood between the stop cuts by gently pushing the knife into the wood and lifting out small chips of wood.

Maintaining Control: Use controlled pressure and steady hand movements to guide the knife along the marked line, removing wood evenly to create a straight-walled groove. Keep the blade of the knife sharp to ensure clean cuts and prevent splintering or tearing of the wood fibers.

Adjusting Depth: Control the depth of the cut by adjusting the angle and pressure of the knife. For shallow cuts, use a lighter touch, and for deeper cuts, apply slightly more pressure while maintaining control over the knife.

Refining the Groove: After removing the wood between the stop cuts, use your knife or chisel to clean up any rough edges or imperfections along the edges of the groove. Ensure that the walls of the groove are straight and even, with crisp edges.

Repeat as Needed: Repeat the process for each straight line or border in your design, adjusting the length and spacing of the lines as necessary to create the desired pattern.

Curve Walled Chip

The curve-walled chip is a versatile technique in chip carving, allowing you to create flowing curves and intricate patterns. Here's how to execute the curve-walled chip:

Marking the Design: Begin by marking the outline of the curved line or shape you want to carve onto the wood surface using a pencil or marking knife. Use a compass or template to ensure smooth and symmetrical curves.

Making the Stop Cuts: With your chip carving knife, make two shallow cuts along the length of the marked curve, defining the edges of the chip. These cuts are known as the "stop cuts" and serve as boundaries for the chip.

Creating the Curved Wall: Position your knife at a slight angle to the wood surface, with the cutting edge facing towards the center of the marked curve. Begin removing wood between the stop cuts by gently pushing the knife into the wood and lifting out small chips of wood.

Following the Curve: Use controlled pressure and steady hand movements to guide the knife along the marked curve, following its contours closely. Keep the blade of the knife sharp to ensure clean cuts and smooth curves.

Adjusting Depth: Control the depth of the cut by adjusting the angle and pressure of the knife. For shallow curves, use a lighter touch, and for deeper curves, apply slightly more pressure while maintaining control over the knife.

Refining the Curve: After removing the wood between the stop cuts, use your knife or chisel to clean up any rough edges or imperfections along the edges of the curve. Ensure that the curve is smooth and flowing, with crisp edges.

Repeat as Needed: Repeat the process for each curved line or shape in your design, adjusting the length and spacing of the curves as necessary to create the desired pattern.

Incised Chip

The incised chip technique in chip carving allows for creating depth and adding texture to your designs. Here's how to execute the incised chip:

Marking the Design: Begin by marking the outline of the area you want to carve onto the wood surface using a pencil or marking knife. This will define the boundaries of your incised chip design.

Making the Stop Cuts: Use a chip carving knife or chisel to make shallow stop cuts along the outline of the design. These cuts will help define the edges of the chip and prevent the wood from splitting beyond the desired area.

Creating Incisions: With the tip of your carving knife or a veining tool, make vertical incisions within the outlined area of the design. These incisions should be made at varying depths to create a textured effect, with some cuts being shallower than others.

Removing Wood: Once the incisions are made, use the tip of your carving knife or a small gouge to carefully remove small chips of wood from between the incisions. Work slowly and cautiously to avoid damaging the surrounding wood and to control the depth of the cuts.

Refining the Texture: After removing the wood between the incisions, use a small gouge or V-tool to refine the texture of the incised area. You can deepen some of the incisions or add additional texture as desired to enhance the overall effect.

Smoothing the Surface: Once the incised chip design is complete, use sandpaper or a fine-grit abrasive to smooth the surrounding wood surface. This will help blend the incised area with the rest of the wood and create a seamless finish.

Finish and Seal: Finally, apply a finish or sealer to the carved surface to protect the wood and enhance its appearance. Choose a finish that complements the wood species and desired aesthetic of your project.

Adding Texture And Depth

Adding texture and depth to chip carving designs can elevate them from simple patterns to intricate works of art. Here are several techniques for achieving texture and depth in your chip carving projects:

Varying Depths: Carve sections of your design at different depths to create visual interest and depth. Use deeper cuts for foreground elements and shallower cuts for background areas to create a sense of depth and dimension.

Incised Lines: Use a chip carving knife or V-tool to make incised lines within your design. Vary the depth and spacing of the lines to create texture and add visual interest to the carved surface.

Relief Carving: Combine chip carving with relief carving techniques to create three-dimensional effects. Carve some elements of your design in low relief (raised slightly from the surface) to add depth and dimension to your carving.

Background Removal: Carve away the background around your design to create a raised or recessed effect. This technique can create a sense of depth and make your design stand out from the surrounding wood surface.

Textured Backgrounds: Use stippling, punching, or texturing tools to create a textured background behind your chip-carved design. This can add visual interest and contrast to your carving and enhance the overall composition.

Undercutting: Make undercutting cuts beneath certain elements of your design to create shadow and depth. This technique involves carving away the wood beneath the surface to create a recessed area, adding depth and dimension to the carving.

Layering Chips: Instead of removing all the wood from a particular area, leave some chips partially attached to create a layered effect. Vary the depth and angle of the chips to create texture and depth within the design.

Burnishing and Highlighting: After carving, use a burnishing tool or fine-grit sandpaper to smooth the surface of the carved areas. This can help highlight the texture and depth of the carving by creating contrast between the raised and recessed areas.

Shading and Highlighting

Shading and highlighting are essential techniques in chip carving that can enhance the depth, dimension, and visual impact of your designs. Here's how to effectively shade and highlight your chip carving projects:

Study Light and Shadow: Before you begin carving, take some time to study how light interacts with different surfaces and objects. Understanding the principles of light and shadow will help you identify areas of your design that should be shaded or highlighted to create realistic and dynamic effects.

Plan Your Design: Consider the light source and the direction of light when planning your chip carving design. Imagine where shadows would naturally fall and where highlights would appear on the carved surface. This will help you determine which areas of your design should be shaded and highlighted for a realistic effect.

Gradual Shading: Use your chip carving knife or gouge to gradually deepen the cuts in areas where shadows would naturally occur. Start with shallow cuts and gradually increase the depth to create a smooth transition from light to shadow.

Cross-Hatching: Cross-hatching is a shading technique where you make a series of closely spaced parallel cuts in one direction, then make another series of parallel cuts in a different direction to create a cross-hatched pattern. This technique can be used to create subtle shading and add depth to your carving.

Highlighting: Use your chip carving knife or gouge to make shallow cuts or remove small chips of wood in areas where light would hit the surface of your carving. This will create highlights and add brightness to the design, making it appear more three-dimensional.

Use Contrast: Contrast is key to creating realistic shading and highlighting effects. Make sure there is a noticeable difference in depth and tone between shaded areas and highlighted areas to create a sense of volume and dimension.

Blend and Smooth: After carving, use sandpaper or a fine-grit abrasive to smooth the surface of your carving and blend the shaded and highlighted areas together. This will create a seamless transition between light and shadow and enhance the overall realism of your design.

Experiment and Practice: Shading and highlighting are skills that improve with practice and experimentation. Take the time to experiment with different techniques and approaches to find what works best for your carving style and the effect you want to achieve.

Creating Three Dimensional Effects

Creating three-dimensional effects in chip carving involves using carving techniques to give the illusion of depth and dimensionality within a flat surface. Here are several techniques to achieve three-dimensional effects in chip carving:

Relief Carving: Relief carving entails sculpting designs that protrude from the surface, producing a captivating three-dimensional impression. Carve certain elements of your design in higher relief (raised above the surface) to add depth and dimension to your carving. This can be achieved by gradually carving away the background while leaving the raised elements intact.

Layering Chips: Instead of removing all the wood from a particular area, leave some chips partially attached to create a layered effect. Vary the depth and angle of the chips to create texture and depth within the design, giving the illusion of multiple layers or levels.

Undercutting: Make undercutting cuts beneath certain elements of your design to create shadow and depth. This technique involves carving away the wood beneath the surface to create a recessed area, adding depth and dimension to the carving. By carving deeper into the wood in certain areas, you can create the illusion of shadows and make those elements appear farther back in space.

Graduated Depth: Use carving tools to gradually deepen the cuts in areas where shadows would naturally occur, such as along the edges of objects or in recessed areas. Start with shallow cuts and gradually increase the depth to create a smooth transition from light to shadow, giving the illusion of depth and volume.

Highlighting and Shading: Use shading and highlighting techniques to create the illusion of light and shadow on the carved surface. Carve certain areas deeper to create shadows, and carve other areas shallower to create highlights. This will add depth and dimension to your carving and make it appear more three-dimensional.

Texturing: Use texturing tools or techniques to add texture and dimension to your carving. This can involve creating patterns or textures within the design, such as wood grain, fur, or fabric texture, to give the illusion of depth and tactile detail.

Contrast: Contrast is key to creating three-dimensional effects in chip carving. Make sure there is a noticeable difference in depth and tone between the raised elements and the background to create a sense of volume and dimension.

CHAPTER FOUR
Finishing and Refining

Sanding And Smoothing
Sanding and smoothing are crucial steps in chip carving to achieve a polished and professional finish. Here's a guide to sanding and smoothing your chip-carved projects effectively:

Start with Coarse Grit Sandpaper: Begin sanding with coarse grit sandpaper (around 120 grit) to remove any rough spots, tool marks, or imperfections from the surface of your carving. Sand in the direction of the wood grain using smooth, even strokes to avoid creating scratches or gouges.

Progress to Finer Grits: Gradually progress to finer grit sandpaper as you refine the surface of your carving. Move through progressively higher grits, such as 180, 220, and 320 grit, to achieve a smoother and more polished finish. Each successive grit will help to remove scratches and refine the surface further.

Use Sanding Blocks or Pads: To ensure even sanding and prevent uneven surfaces, use sanding blocks or pads to support the sandpaper. This will help distribute pressure evenly and prevent over-sanding in certain areas.

Sand Curved Areas Carefully: Pay special attention to curved or intricate areas of your carving, as these may require more careful sanding to avoid rounding over sharp edges or details. Use smaller pieces of sandpaper or sanding sticks to reach into tight spaces and crevices.

Check for Consistency: Periodically inspect your carving for consistency in texture and smoothness as you sand. Look for any remaining tool marks, scratches, or uneven areas that may need further attention.

Remove Dust: After sanding with each grit, use a clean, dry brush or cloth to remove any sanding dust from the surface of your carving. This will help you see your progress and prevent the buildup of dust particles on the wood surface.

Finish with Fine Grits: Finish sanding with the finest grit sandpaper available to achieve a smooth and polished surface. Optionally, you can wet-sand your carving with a fine-grit sandpaper (400 grit or higher) to further refine the surface and remove any remaining imperfections.

Inspect and Touch Up: Once sanding is complete, carefully inspect your carving for any remaining imperfections or rough spots. Use finer sandpaper or sanding sticks to touch up any areas that need additional smoothing or refining.

Apply Finish: After sanding and smoothing your carving to your satisfaction, apply a finish or sealant to protect the wood and enhance its appearance. Choose a finish that complements the wood species and desired aesthetic of your project, such as oil-based varnish, shellac, or polyurethane.

Applying Finishing Touches

Applying finishing touches is the final step in completing your chip carving project and giving it that polished and professional look. Here are some suggestions for incorporating those finishing touches:

Inspect Your Carving: Before applying any finishing touches, carefully inspect your carving for any imperfections or areas that may need touch-ups. Look for any stray marks, rough spots, or uneven areas that could detract from the overall appearance of your carving.

Touch-Up Carving: Use carving tools or sandpaper to touch up any areas of your carving that may need refinement. Smooth out any rough spots, sharpen edges, and ensure that all details are crisp and well-defined.

Apply a Finish: Choose an appropriate finish for your carving based on the wood species and desired look. Common finishes for chip carving projects include oil-based varnish, shellac, polyurethane, or a combination of wax and oil. Apply the finish according to the manufacturer's instructions, using a brush, cloth, or foam applicator.

Enhance Contrast: If desired, use a wood stain or dye to enhance the contrast between the carved areas and the surrounding wood. Apply the stain or dye carefully to avoid staining areas you don't want colored, and wipe off any excess with a clean cloth.

Highlight Details: Consider adding highlights to certain areas of your carving to make them stand out more. This can be done by lightly sanding or burnishing raised areas, applying a lighter-colored stain or paint, or using a wood-burning tool to add accents.

Protect the Back: If your carving will be displayed or handled frequently, consider adding a protective backing to the back of the piece. This can help prevent damage to the wood and provide a finished look to the back of the carving.

Sign Your Work: Finally, consider signing or initialing your carving to add a personal touch and indicate that it is your original work. You can do this by carving your initials into the wood, adding a small plaque or label, or signing the back of the carving with a permanent marker.

Repairing Mistakes

Repairing mistakes in chip carving requires patience and precision to restore the integrity of the carving without compromising its overall appearance. Here are some steps you can take to address common mistakes:

Assess the Damage: Take a close look at the mistake to determine the extent of the damage. Identify whether it's a minor flaw that can be easily fixed or a more significant error that requires more extensive repair.

Evaluate Options: Depending on the nature of the mistake, you may have several options for repair. For minor errors such as small chips or nicks, you may be able to sand or carve away the damaged area and blend it into the surrounding wood. For more significant mistakes, you may need to fill in the area with wood filler or epoxy before sanding and refinishing.

Sand and Smooth: If the mistake is minor and localized, carefully sand the affected area to remove any rough edges or imperfections. Use progressively finer grit sandpaper to blend the repaired area into the surrounding wood, ensuring a smooth and seamless finish.

Fill and Patch: For larger or more noticeable mistakes, consider filling in the damaged area with wood filler or epoxy. Choose a filler that matches the color and grain of the surrounding wood as closely as possible. Apply the filler according to the manufacturer's instructions, then sand and smooth the repaired area once it has cured.

Carve and Recarve: In some cases, you may need to carve away the damaged area and recarve the design from scratch. This approach is more time-consuming but may be necessary for mistakes that cannot be easily repaired using other methods. Use your carving tools to carefully remove the damaged wood and recreate the design as accurately as possible.

Blend and Finish: Once the repair is complete, take the time to blend the repaired area into the surrounding wood and ensure a seamless transition between the repaired section and the rest of the carving. Sand the entire surface of the carving to achieve a uniform finish, then apply a finish or sealant to protect the wood and enhance its appearance.

Learn from Mistakes: Finally, take the opportunity to learn from your mistakes and use them as valuable learning experiences. Analyze what went wrong and how you can avoid similar mistakes in the future, whether it's adjusting your carving technique, using sharper tools, or taking more time to plan and execute your designs.

CHAPTER FIVE
Projects For Practice

Beginner Projects

Chip Carved Coaster

Materials Needed:

- Basswood square blank (4"x4"x1/4")
- Chip carving knife
- Pencil
- Sandpaper in varying grits: 120, 220, and 320.
- Finish (optional)

Step-by-Step Guide:

Design Planning: Sketch a simple geometric design onto the surface of the basswood square blank using a pencil. Consider using basic shapes like triangles, squares, or diamonds for your design.

Transfer the Design: Once you're happy with your design, use transfer paper or carbon paper to transfer the design onto the wood surface. Press firmly to ensure the lines are transferred clearly.

Make Stop Cuts: With your chip carving knife, carefully make shallow stop cuts along the outlines of your design. These stop cuts will define the edges of your chips and help prevent splintering.

Chip Carving: Begin chip carving by removing small triangular chips of wood from within the outlines of your design. Start with the centermost chips and work your way outwards, using the stop cuts as guidelines.

Refine the Design: After removing the chips, use your chip carving knife to clean up any rough edges or imperfections in the design. Pay attention to detail and ensure each chip is clean and crisp.

Sand the Surface: Once carving is complete, sand the entire surface of the coaster with progressively finer grits of sandpaper (120 grit, 220 grit, and 320 grit) to smooth out the wood surface and remove any tool marks.

Apply Finish (Optional): If desired, apply a finish or sealant to the surface of the coaster to protect the wood and enhance its appearance. Allow the finish to dry completely before using the coaster.

Chip Carved Keychain

Materials Needed:

- Basswood keychain blank

- Chip carving knife
- Pencil
- Sandpaper in varying grits: 120, 220, and 320.
- Keychain hardware
- Finish (optional)

Step-by-Step Guide:

Design Planning: Sketch a simple design onto the surface of the basswood keychain blank using a pencil. Consider using initials, a small motif, or a geometric pattern for your design.

Transfer the Design: Use transfer paper or carbon paper to transfer the design onto the wood surface. Press firmly to ensure the lines are transferred clearly.

Make Stop Cuts: With your chip carving knife, carefully make shallow stop cuts along the outlines of your design. These stop cuts will define the edges of your chips and help prevent splintering.

Chip Carving: Begin chip carving by removing small triangular chips of wood from within the outlines of your design. Start with the centermost chips and work your way outwards, using the stop cuts as guidelines.

Refine the Design: After removing the chips, use your chip carving knife to clean up any rough edges or imperfections in the design. Pay attention to detail and ensure each chip is clean and crisp.

Shape the Keychain: Use your chip carving knife to carefully shape the edges and corners of the keychain blank into a rounded or beveled shape, if desired.

Sand the Surface: Once carving is complete, sand the entire surface of the keychain with progressively finer grits of sandpaper (120 grit, 220 grit, and 320 grit) to smooth out the wood surface and remove any tool marks.

Apply Finish (Optional): If desired, apply a finish or sealant to the surface of the keychain to protect the wood and enhance its appearance. Allow the finish to dry completely before attaching the keychain hardware.

Attach Keychain Hardware: Finally, attach the keychain hardware to the top of the keychain blank using a small screwdriver or glue, following the manufacturer's instructions.

Chip Carved Decorative Spoon

Materials Needed:

- Basswood spoon blank
- Chip carving knife
- Pencil
- Sandpaper in varying grits: 120, 220, and 320.
- Finish (food-safe if intended for use)

Step-by-Step Guide:

Design Planning: Sketch a simple design onto the handle of the basswood spoon blank using a pencil. Consider using geometric patterns, swirls, or small motifs for your design.

Transfer the Design: Use transfer paper or carbon paper to transfer the design onto the wood surface of the spoon handle. Ensure the lines are transferred clearly and accurately.

Make Stop Cuts: With your chip carving knife, carefully make shallow stop cuts along the outlines of your design. These stop cuts will define the edges of your chips and help prevent splintering.

Chip Carving: Begin chip carving by removing small triangular chips of wood from within the outlines of your design. Start with the centermost chips and work your way outwards, using the stop cuts as guidelines.

Refine the Design: After removing the chips, use your chip carving knife to clean up any rough edges or imperfections in the design. Pay attention to detail and ensure each chip is clean and crisp.

Shape the Spoon: Use your chip carving knife to carefully shape the edges and contours of the spoon handle, if desired. You can round off edges or add decorative grooves to enhance the design.

Sand the Surface: Once carving is complete, sand the entire surface of the spoon with progressively finer grits of sandpaper (120 grit, 220 grit, and 320 grit) to smooth out the wood surface and remove any tool marks.

Apply Finish: If the spoon will be used for food, apply a food-safe finish such as mineral oil or beeswax to protect the wood and enhance its appearance. If the spoon is purely decorative, you can use a wood finish of your choice.

Chip Carved Personalized Wooden Plaque

Materials Needed:

- Basswood plaque blank
- Chip carving knife
- Pencil
- Sandpaper in varying grits: 120, 220, and 320.
- Woodburning tool (optional)
- Finish (optional)

Step-by-Step Guide:

Design Planning: Sketch the outline of the plaque and any desired text or motifs onto the surface of the basswood plaque blank using a pencil. Plan the layout and spacing of your design carefully.

Transfer the Design: Use transfer paper or carbon paper to transfer the design onto the wood surface of the plaque. Ensure the lines are transferred clearly and accurately.

Make Stop Cuts: With your chip carving knife, carefully make shallow stop cuts along the outlines of your design. These stop cuts will define the edges of your chips and help prevent splintering.

Chip Carving: Begin chip carving by removing small triangular chips of wood from within the outlines of your design.

Start with the centermost chips and work your way outwards, using the stop cuts as guidelines.

Refine the Design: After removing the chips, use your chip carving knife to clean up any rough edges or imperfections in the design. Pay attention to detail and ensure each chip is clean and crisp.

Add Woodburning (Optional): If desired, use a woodburning tool to add additional details or text to your plaque. This can be especially useful for adding fine lines or intricate patterns that may be difficult to achieve with chip carving alone.

Sand the Surface: Once carving and woodburning (if applicable) are complete, sand the entire surface of the plaque with progressively finer grits of sandpaper (120 grit, 220 grit, and 320 grit) to smooth out the wood surface and remove any tool marks.

Apply Finish (Optional): If desired, apply a finish or sealant to the surface of the plaque to protect the wood and enhance its appearance. Choose a finish that complements the wood species and desired aesthetic of your project.

Chip Carved Decorative Wooden Box

Materials Needed:

- Basswood box blank
- Chip carving knife
- Pencil
- Sandpaper in varying grits: 120, 220, and 320.
- Finish (optional)

Step-by-Step Guide:

Design Planning: Sketch a simple design onto the lid or sides of the basswood box blank using a pencil. Consider using geometric patterns, floral motifs, or abstract designs for your carving.

Transfer the Design: Use transfer paper or carbon paper to transfer the design onto the wood surface of the box. Ensure the lines are transferred clearly and accurately.

Make Stop Cuts: With your chip carving knife, carefully make shallow stop cuts along the outlines of your design. These stop cuts will define the edges of your chips and help prevent splintering.

Chip Carving: Begin chip carving by removing small triangular chips of wood from within the outlines of your design. Start with the centermost chips and work your way outwards, using the stop cuts as guidelines.

Refine the Design: After removing the chips, use your chip carving knife to clean up any rough edges or imperfections in the design. Pay attention to detail and ensure each chip is clean and crisp.

Shape the Box (Optional): Use your chip carving knife to carefully shape the edges and contours of the box, if desired. You can round off edges or add decorative grooves to enhance the design.

Sand the Surface: Once carving is complete, sand the entire surface of the box with progressively finer grits of sandpaper (120 grit, 220 grit, and 320 grit) to smooth out the wood surface and remove any tool marks.

Apply Finish (Optional): If desired, apply a finish or sealant to the surface of the box to protect the wood and enhance its appearance. Choose a finish that complements the wood species and desired aesthetic of your project.

Chip Carved Personalized Key Holder

Materials Needed:

- Basswood plaque blank
- Chip carving knife

- Pencil
- Sandpaper in varying grits: 120, 220, and 320.
- Key hooks
- Wood stain or finish (optional)

Step-by-Step Guide:

Design Planning: Sketch the outline of the plaque and any desired text or motifs onto the surface of the basswood plaque blank using a pencil. Plan the layout and spacing of your design carefully, leaving space for the key hooks.

Transfer the Design: Use transfer paper or carbon paper to transfer the design onto the wood surface of the plaque. Ensure the lines are transferred clearly and accurately.

Make Stop Cuts: With your chip carving knife, carefully make shallow stop cuts along the outlines of your design and around the areas where the key hooks will be attached. These stop cuts will define the edges of your chips and help prevent splintering.

Chip Carving: Begin chip carving by removing small triangular chips of wood from within the outlines of your design. Start with the centermost chips and work your way outwards, using the stop cuts as guidelines.

Refine the Design: After removing the chips, use your chip carving knife to clean up any rough edges or imperfections in the design. Pay attention to detail and ensure each chip is clean and crisp.

Attach Key Hooks: Once carving is complete and the wood surface is smooth, attach key hooks to the bottom of the plaque using screws or glue, following the manufacturer's instructions.

Sand the Surface: Sand the entire surface of the plaque with progressively finer grits of sandpaper (120 grit, 220 grit, and 320 grit) to smooth out the wood surface and remove any tool marks.

Apply Finish (Optional): If desired, apply a wood stain or finish to the surface of the plaque to protect the wood and enhance its appearance. Allow the finish to dry completely before using the key holder.

Intermediate Projects

Chip Carved Decorative Wooden Bowl

Materials Needed:

- Basswood bowl blank
- Chip carving knife
- Pencil
- Sandpaper in varying grits: 120, 220, and 320.
- Finish (food-safe if intended for use)

Step-by-Step Guide:

Design Planning: Sketch a simple design onto the outer rim or sides of the basswood bowl blank using a pencil. Consider using geometric patterns, nature-inspired motifs, or intricate designs for your carving.

Transfer the Design: Use transfer paper or carbon paper to transfer the design onto the wood surface of the bowl. Ensure the lines are transferred clearly and accurately.

Make Stop Cuts: With your chip carving knife, carefully make shallow stop cuts along the outlines of your design. These stop cuts will define the edges of your chips and help prevent splintering.

Chip Carving: Begin chip carving by removing small triangular chips of wood from within the outlines of your design. Start with the centermost chips and work your way outwards, using the stop cuts as guidelines.

Refine the Design: After removing the chips, use your chip carving knife to clean up any rough edges or imperfections in the design. Pay attention to detail and ensure each chip is clean and crisp.

Shape the Bowl: Use your chip carving knife to carefully shape the outer rim or sides of the bowl, if desired. You can round off edges or add decorative grooves to enhance the design.

Sand the Surface: Once carving is complete, sand the entire surface of the bowl with progressively finer grits of sandpaper (120 grit, 220 grit, and 320 grit) to smooth out the wood surface and remove any tool marks.

Apply Finish: If the bowl will be used for food, apply a food-safe finish such as mineral oil or beeswax to protect the wood and enhance its appearance. If the bowl is purely decorative, you can use a wood finish of your choice.

Chip Carved Picture Frame

Materials Needed:

- Basswood picture frame blank
- Chip carving knife
- Pencil
- Sandpaper in varying grits: 120, 220, and 320.
- Picture or photo to fit the frame
- Finish (optional)

Step-by-Step Guide:

Design Planning: Sketch a simple design onto the outer edges of the basswood picture frame blank using a pencil. Consider using geometric patterns, floral motifs, or personalized initials for your carving.

Transfer the Design: Use transfer paper or carbon paper to transfer the design onto the wood surface of the frame. Ensure the lines are transferred clearly and accurately.

Make Stop Cuts: With your chip carving knife, carefully make shallow stop cuts along the outlines of your design. These stop cuts will define the edges of your chips and help prevent splintering.

Chip Carving: Begin chip carving by removing small triangular chips of wood from within the outlines of your design. Start with the centermost chips and work your way outwards, using the stop cuts as guidelines.

Refine the Design: After removing the chips, use your chip carving knife to clean up any rough edges or imperfections in the design. Pay attention to detail and ensure each chip is clean and crisp.

Sand the Surface: Once carving is complete, sand the entire surface of the picture frame with progressively finer grits of sandpaper (120 grit, 220 grit, and 320 grit) to smooth out the wood surface and remove any tool marks.

Fit the Picture: Insert a picture or photo into the frame that fits the dimensions of the opening. Ensure the picture is centered and secure within the frame.

Apply Finish (Optional): If desired, apply a finish or sealant to the surface of the frame to protect the wood and enhance its appearance. Choose a finish that complements the wood species and desired aesthetic of your project.

Chip Carved Decorative Serving Tray

Materials Needed:

- Wooden serving tray blank
- Chip carving knife
- Pencil
- Sandpaper in varying grits: 120, 220, and 320.
- Finish (food-safe if intended for use)

Step-by-Step Guide:

Design Planning: Sketch a decorative design onto the surface of the wooden serving tray blank using a pencil. Consider incorporating geometric patterns, floral motifs, or abstract designs for your carving.

Transfer the Design: Use transfer paper or carbon paper to transfer the design onto the wood surface of the serving tray. Ensure the lines are transferred clearly and accurately.

Make Stop Cuts: With your chip carving knife, carefully make shallow stop cuts along the outlines of your design. These stop cuts will define the edges of your chips and help prevent splintering.

Chip Carving: Begin chip carving by removing small triangular chips of wood from within the outlines of your design. Start with the centermost chips and work your way outwards, using the stop cuts as guidelines.

Refine the Design: After removing the chips, use your chip carving knife to clean up any rough edges or imperfections in the design. Pay attention to detail and ensure each chip is clean and crisp.

Sand the Surface: Once carving is complete, sand the entire surface of the serving tray with progressively finer grits of sandpaper (120 grit, 220 grit, and 320 grit) to smooth out the wood surface and remove any tool marks.

Apply Finish: If the serving tray will be used for food, apply a food-safe finish such as mineral oil or beeswax to protect the wood and enhance its appearance. If the tray is purely decorative, you can use a wood finish of your choice.

Chip Carved Box with Hinged Lid

Materials Needed:

- Wooden box with hinged lid
- Chip carving knife
- Pencil
- Sandpaper in varying grits: 120, 220, and 320.
- Finish (optional)

Step-by-Step Guide:

Design Planning: Sketch a decorative design onto the surface of the wooden box and lid using a pencil. Consider using geometric patterns, nature-inspired motifs, or personalized initials for your carving.

Transfer the Design: Use transfer paper or carbon paper to transfer the design onto the wood surface of the box and lid. Ensure the lines are transferred clearly and accurately.

Make Stop Cuts: With your chip carving knife, carefully make shallow stop cuts along the outlines of your design. These stop cuts will define the edges of your chips and help prevent splintering.

Chip Carving: Begin chip carving by removing small triangular chips of wood from within the outlines of your design. Start with the centermost chips and work your way outwards, using the stop cuts as guidelines.

Refine the Design: After removing the chips, use your chip carving knife to clean up any rough edges or imperfections in the design. Pay attention to detail and ensure each chip is clean and crisp.

Sand the Surface: Once carving is complete, sand the entire surface of the box and lid with progressively finer grits of sandpaper (120 grit, 220 grit, and 320 grit) to smooth out the wood surface and remove any tool marks.

Apply Finish (Optional): If desired, apply a finish or sealant to the surface of the box and lid to protect the wood and enhance its appearance. Choose a finish that complements the wood species and desired aesthetic of your project.

Advanced Projects

Chip Carved Wooden Jewelry Box

Materials Needed:

- Wooden jewelry box blank with multiple compartments
- Chip carving knife
- Pencil
- Sandpaper in varying grits: 120, 220, and 320.
- Hinges and clasp (optional)
- Finish (optional)

Step-by-Step Guide:

Design Planning: Sketch a detailed and intricate design onto the lid and sides of the wooden jewelry box blank using a pencil. Consider incorporating geometric patterns, floral motifs, or personalized initials for your carving.

Transfer the Design: Use transfer paper or carbon paper to transfer the design onto the wood surface of the jewelry box. Ensure the lines are transferred clearly and accurately.

Make Stop Cuts: With your chip carving knife, carefully make shallow stop cuts along the outlines of your design. These stop cuts will define the edges of your chips and help prevent splintering.

Chip Carving: Begin chip carving by removing small triangular chips of wood from within the outlines of your design. Work slowly and meticulously, paying attention to detail and ensuring each chip is clean and crisp.

Refine the Design: After removing the chips, use your chip carving knife to clean up any rough edges or imperfections in the design. Take your time to achieve a high level of detail and precision in your carving.

Shape the Box (Optional): Use your chip carving knife to carefully shape the edges and contours of the jewelry box, if desired. You can round off edges or add decorative grooves to enhance the design.

Sand the Surface: Once carving is complete, sand the entire surface of the jewelry box with progressively finer grits of sandpaper (120 grit, 220 grit, and 320 grit) to smooth out the wood surface and remove any tool marks.

Attach Hinges and Clasp (Optional): If desired, attach hinges and a clasp to the jewelry box to create a functional and decorative piece. Follow the manufacturer's instructions for installation.

Apply Finish (Optional): If desired, apply a finish or sealant to the surface of the jewelry box to protect the wood and enhance its appearance. Choose a finish that complements the wood species and desired aesthetic of your project.

Chip Carved Decorative Panel

Materials Needed:

- Basswood panel blank
- Chip carving knife
- Pencil
- Sandpaper in varying grits: 120, 220, and 320.
- Stain or finish (optional)

Step-by-Step Guide:

Design Planning: Sketch a large and intricate design onto the surface of the basswood panel blank using a pencil. Consider creating a scene, pattern, or abstract composition for your carving.

Transfer the Design: Use transfer paper or carbon paper to transfer the design onto the wood surface of the panel. Ensure the lines are transferred clearly and accurately.

Make Stop Cuts: With your chip carving knife, carefully make shallow stop cuts along the outlines of your design. These stop cuts will define the edges of your chips and help prevent splintering.

Chip Carving: Begin chip carving by removing small triangular chips of wood from within the outlines of your design. Work slowly and methodically, paying close attention to detail and achieving a high level of precision.

Refine the Design: After removing the chips, use your chip carving knife to clean up any rough edges or imperfections in the design. Take your time to ensure each chip is clean and crisp, and the overall design is well-defined.

Sand the Surface: Once carving is complete, sand the entire surface of the panel with progressively finer grits of sandpaper (120 grit, 220 grit, and 320 grit) to smooth out the wood surface and remove any tool marks.

Stain or Finish (Optional): If desired, apply a wood stain or finish to the surface of the panel to enhance the wood grain and protect the carving. Choose a stain or finish that complements the wood species and desired aesthetic of your project.

Chip Carved Decorative Clock

Materials Needed:

- Wooden clock blank
- Chip carving knife
- Pencil
- Clock mechanism
- Sandpaper in varying grits: 120, 220, and 320.
- Finish (optional)

Step-by-Step Guide:

Design Planning: Sketch a detailed and intricate design onto the face of the wooden clock blank using a pencil. Consider incorporating geometric patterns, swirls, or personalized motifs for your carving.

Transfer the Design: Use transfer paper or carbon paper to transfer the design onto the wood surface of the clock blank. Ensure the lines are transferred clearly and accurately.

Make Stop Cuts: With your chip carving knife, carefully make shallow stop cuts along the outlines of your design. These stop cuts will define the edges of your chips and help prevent splintering.

Chip Carving: Begin chip carving by removing small triangular chips of wood from within the outlines of your design. Work meticulously, paying close attention to detail and achieving a high level of precision.

Refine the Design: After removing the chips, use your chip carving knife to clean up any rough edges or imperfections in the design. Take your time to ensure each chip is clean and crisp, and the overall design is well-defined.

Shape the Clock (Optional): Use your chip carving knife to carefully shape the edges and contours of the clock, if desired. You can round off edges or add decorative grooves to enhance the design.

Install Clock Mechanism: Follow the manufacturer's instructions to install the clock mechanism into the center of the clock face. Ensure the mechanism is securely attached and functional.

Sand the Surface: Once carving is complete, sand the entire surface of the clock with progressively finer grits of sandpaper (120 grit, 220 grit, and 320 grit) to smooth out the wood surface and remove any tool marks.

Apply Finish (Optional): If desired, apply a finish or sealant to the surface of the clock to protect the wood and enhance its appearance. Choose a finish that complements the wood species and desired aesthetic of your project.

Chip Carved Wall Plaque with Relief Design

Materials Needed:

- Basswood panel blank

- Chip carving knife
- Pencil
- Sandpaper in varying grits: 120, 220, and 320.
- Stain or finish (optional)

Step-by-Step Guide:

Design Planning: Sketch a detailed and intricate relief design onto the surface of the basswood panel blank using a pencil. Consider creating a scene, portrait, or abstract composition for your carving.

Transfer the Design: Use transfer paper or carbon paper to transfer the design onto the wood surface of the panel. Ensure the lines are transferred clearly and accurately.

Make Stop Cuts: With your chip carving knife, carefully make shallow stop cuts along the outlines of your design. These stop cuts will define the edges of your relief carving and help prevent splintering.

Chip Carving: Begin chip carving by removing small triangular chips of wood from within the outlines of your design. Work slowly and methodically, paying close attention to detail and achieving a high level of precision.

Build Up Relief: Gradually build up the relief by carving deeper into the wood and creating layers of depth within the design. Use your chip carving knife to carefully shape and contour the relief to bring the design to life.

Refine the Design: After carving the relief, use your chip carving knife to clean up any rough edges or imperfections in the design. Take your time to ensure each detail is clean and crisp.

Sand the Surface: Once carving is complete, sand the entire surface of the panel with progressively finer grits of sandpaper (120 grit, 220 grit, and 320 grit) to smooth out the wood surface and remove any tool marks.

Stain or Finish (Optional): If desired, apply a wood stain or finish to the surface of the panel to enhance the wood grain and protect the carving. Choose a stain or finish that complements the wood species and desired aesthetic of your project.

Chip Carved Decorative Mirror Frame

Materials Needed:

- Wooden mirror frame blank
- Chip carving knife
- Pencil
- Mirror
- Sandpaper in varying grits: 120, 220, and 320.
- Finish (optional)

Step-by-Step Guide:

Design Planning: Sketch a detailed and intricate design onto the surface of the wooden mirror frame blank using a pencil. Consider incorporating geometric patterns, floral motifs, or personalized initials for your carving.

Transfer the Design: Use transfer paper or carbon paper to transfer the design onto the wood surface of the mirror frame. Ensure the lines are transferred clearly and accurately.

Make Stop Cuts: With your chip carving knife, carefully make shallow stop cuts along the outlines of your design. These stop cuts will define the edges of your chips and help prevent splintering.

Chip Carving: Begin chip carving by removing small triangular chips of wood from within the outlines of your design. Work meticulously, paying close attention to detail and achieving a high level of precision.

Refine the Design: After removing the chips, use your chip carving knife to clean up any rough edges or imperfections in the design. Take your time to ensure each chip is clean and crisp, and the overall design is well-defined.

Prepare the Mirror: If necessary, remove any existing mirror from the frame.

Thoroughly clean the frame to eliminate any dust or debris.

Attach the Mirror: Place the mirror into the frame and secure it using mirror adhesive or mounting clips, following the manufacturer's instructions.

Sand the Surface: Once carving is complete, sand the entire surface of the mirror frame with progressively finer grits of sandpaper (120 grit, 220 grit, and 320 grit) to smooth out the wood surface and remove any tool marks.

Apply Finish (Optional): If desired, apply a finish or sealant to the surface of the mirror frame to protect the wood and enhance its appearance. Choose a finish that complements the wood species and desired aesthetic of your project.

Chip Carved Chessboard

Materials Needed:

- Wooden chessboard blank (squares pre-cut or solid wood to create the board)
- Chip carving knife
- Pencil
- Sandpaper in varying grits: 120, 220, and 320.
- Wood stain or finish
- Chess pieces (optional)

Step-by-Step Guide:

Design Planning: Sketch a detailed and intricate checkerboard pattern onto the surface of the wooden chessboard blank using a pencil. Plan the layout carefully, ensuring the squares are evenly sized and spaced.

Transfer the Design: Use transfer paper or carbon paper to transfer the checkerboard pattern onto the wood surface of the chessboard. Ensure the lines are transferred clearly and accurately.

Make Stop Cuts: With your chip carving knife, carefully make shallow stop cuts along the outlines of the checkerboard squares. These stop cuts will define the edges of your chips and help prevent splintering.

Chip Carving: Begin chip carving by removing small triangular chips of wood from within the outlines of the checkerboard squares. Work meticulously, paying close attention to detail and achieving a high level of precision.

Refine the Design: After removing the chips, use your chip carving knife to clean up any rough edges or imperfections in the design. Take your time to ensure each square is clean and crisp, and the overall pattern is well-defined.

Sand the Surface: Once carving is complete, sand the entire surface of the chessboard with progressively finer grits of sandpaper (120 grit, 220 grit, and 320 grit) to smooth out the wood surface and remove any tool marks.

Stain or Finish: Apply a wood stain or finish to the surface of the chessboard to enhance the wood grain and protect the carving. Choose a stain or finish that complements the wood species and desired aesthetic of your project.

Assemble the Chessboard: If the chessboard is not already assembled, arrange the squares in the correct order and glue or nail them into place. Ensure the board is flat and even.

Optional: Complete the chess set by adding chess pieces, either purchased or handcrafted, to complement the chip-carved board.

CHAPTER SIX
Troubleshooting and Tips

Chip carving, like any woodworking technique, can sometimes encounter challenges. Here are some common troubleshooting tips for chip carving:

Uneven Chips: If your chips are uneven or jagged, it could be due to inconsistent pressure while carving. Try to maintain a steady hand and apply even pressure throughout each cut. Additionally, ensure your carving knife is sharp, as dull blades can cause tearing instead of clean cuts.

Splintering: Splintering can occur when making deep cuts or when carving against the grain. To prevent splintering, make sure to carve with the grain whenever possible and make shallow cuts initially, gradually deepening them as needed. You can also use masking tape along the cut lines to minimize splintering.

Wood Tear-out: Tear-out happens when the wood fibers tear instead of cleanly cutting. To minimize tear-out, ensure your carving knife is sharp and make sure to carve with the grain. You can also score the wood lightly along the cut lines before making deeper cuts to help prevent tear-out.

Design Mistakes: If you make a mistake in your design or carving, don't panic. Many mistakes can be fixed by carefully carving away the affected area and refining the surrounding details. Alternatively, you can incorporate the mistake into your design or use wood filler to correct minor errors.

Blade Slipping: Blade slipping can occur if your grip on the carving knife is not secure or if the wood surface is too slick. Make sure to maintain a firm grip on the knife and keep your fingers away from the cutting edge. You can also roughen the wood surface slightly with sandpaper to provide better grip.

Carving Depth: Achieving consistent carving depth can be challenging, especially for intricate designs. Practice controlling the depth of your cuts by making light scoring cuts first and gradually deepening them as needed. Take your time and work slowly to avoid cutting too deeply.

Finishing Issues: If you encounter problems when applying finish to your chip-carved piece, such as uneven coverage or blotching, it may be due to improper surface preparation or application technique. Make sure to sand the surface thoroughly and apply the finish evenly using long, smooth strokes. Allow each coat to dry completely before applying additional coats.

General Tips

Start with the Basics: Begin with simple designs and gradually increase the complexity as you gain confidence and skill. Mastering foundational techniques will set you up for success with more intricate projects.

Use Sharp Tools: Sharp carving tools are essential for clean and precise cuts. Keep your chip carving knife and other tools sharp by regularly honing and sharpening them. Blades that are not sharp enough can result in uneven cuts and cause frustration.

Practice Patience: Chip carving demands patience and meticulous attention to detail. Take your time with each cut and focus on maintaining steady, controlled movements. Rushing can result in mistakes and compromised craftsmanship.

Choose the Right Wood: Select wood species that are suitable for chip carving, such as basswood, butternut, or cherry. These woods have fine, even grain patterns that are conducive to intricate carving. Avoid woods with irregular grain or hardness, as they may be more challenging to carve.

Plan Your Design: Before starting a project, sketch your design on paper to visualize the layout and details. Take into account elements like symmetry, balance, and proportion. Planning ahead will help you execute your design more effectively.

Practice Safety Precautions: Always prioritize safety when chip carving. Wear protective gear like gloves and safety glasses to prevent injuries, and maintain a tidy and organized work area to minimize accidents. Additionally, be mindful of your hand placement and carving direction to minimize the risk of cuts.

Experiment with Techniques: Don't be afraid to experiment with different carving techniques and styles. Try varying the depth and angle of your cuts, incorporating texture, or combining chip carving with other woodworking methods like relief carving or pyrography. Exploring new techniques will broaden your skill set and creativity.

Seek Inspiration: Draw inspiration from chip carving patterns, books, online resources, and fellow woodworkers. Study the work of master carvers and analyze their techniques. Attend workshops or join carving clubs to learn from experienced artisans and exchange ideas with peers.

Embrace Mistakes: Mistakes are a natural part of the learning process. Instead of feeling disheartened, regard mistakes as chances for growth and enhancement.Learn from your errors, adjust your approach, and keep practicing. Over time, you'll become more proficient and confident in your chip carving abilities.

Enjoy the Process: Chip carving is a rewarding and meditative craft that allows you to create beautiful, handcrafted pieces of art. Embrace the journey of carving, savoring each moment of creativity and craftsmanship. Remember to take breaks, step back to admire your progress, and enjoy the satisfaction of bringing your designs to life in wood.

CONCLUSION

Chip carving is a timeless woodworking technique that offers endless opportunities for creativity and expression. Throughout this book, we've explored the rich history, essential tools and materials, safety precautions, and step-by-step techniques for chip carving at various skill levels.

From beginner projects like decorative boxes and key holders to advanced endeavors such as ornate mirror frames and chessboards, chip carving invites woodworkers of all levels to delve into the intricacies of this art form. By practicing patience, honing your skills, and embracing both successes and setbacks, you'll continue to refine your craft and create beautiful, handcrafted pieces that showcase your unique style and vision.

Whether you're carving for relaxation, personal enrichment, or the joy of creation, chip carving offers a fulfilling and rewarding journey. So, pick up your carving knife, select a piece of wood, and let your imagination guide you as you embark on your next chip carving adventure. Remember, the true beauty of chip carving lies not only in the finished product but also in the joy and fulfillment found in the process itself.

Printed in Great Britain
by Amazon